For all the special children who teach us everyday.

Copyright © 2002 The Five Degrees Press

Printed in the United States of America.
For information:
Five Degrees Press
P.O. Box 178
N. Greece, NY 14515
Email Address: ohfrannie@aol.com

Library of Congress Cataloging on
Publication Data
ISBN 0-9679115-5-9

First Printing

Foreward

The Five Degrees Press is a special partnership of women with as many similarities as differences. Collectively, their greatest strength is their spirituality. Through the years, they have experienced the joys and sorrows of life. Each has embraced an inner strength that continues to be a positive force for the team.

Five Degrees Press

Karen Cunico   Finance Coordinator/Editor

Wendy J. Marasco   MIS Coordinator/Editor

Anna Rivoli   Promotion Coordinator/Editor

Linda Ryan   Production Coordinator/Editor

Karen Turkovitz   Author/Editor

Nobody really likes Mitchell. He cries almost everyday for no reason. Everybody knows you don't cry in second grade unless you get cut or something. Not Mitchell. He cries all the time.

He has those kind
of fits that my cousin,
Sammy, has. Aunt Susan
calls them tantrums and
Sammy's got 'em bad!
Aunt Susan says Sammy
will grow out of them
but Mitchell never did.
He still has 'em and
he's seven and a half.

Yesterday Mitchell crawled under his desk and wouldn't come out. Mrs Donley whispered to him but he just covered his face. His ears were as red as the new bicycle I got for my birthday. We

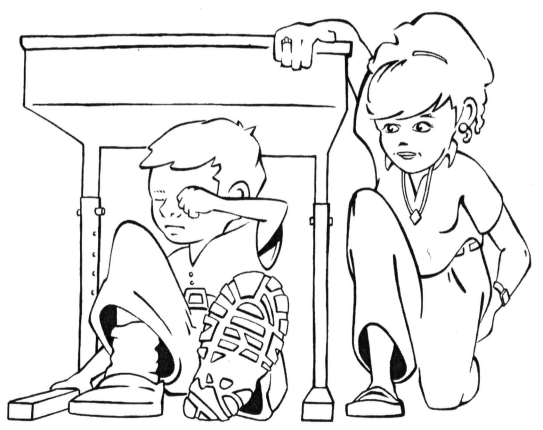

never finished spelling 'cause lots of people kept coming into the room to talk to Mrs. Donley. Some of them tried to get Mitchell out from under the desk but...

... he didn't budge.

Finally, Mrs.Sherman, came
to take Mitchell to her office.
I've never been to Mrs. Sherman's
office. I think you go there if you
have a problem. Mitchell's lucky
'cause he didn't have to take the
math test. He gets stickers for
being good but nobody gives me
stickers, and I'm always good.
Well...except for last Tuesday
when I whispered to Lauren
about her new puppy.

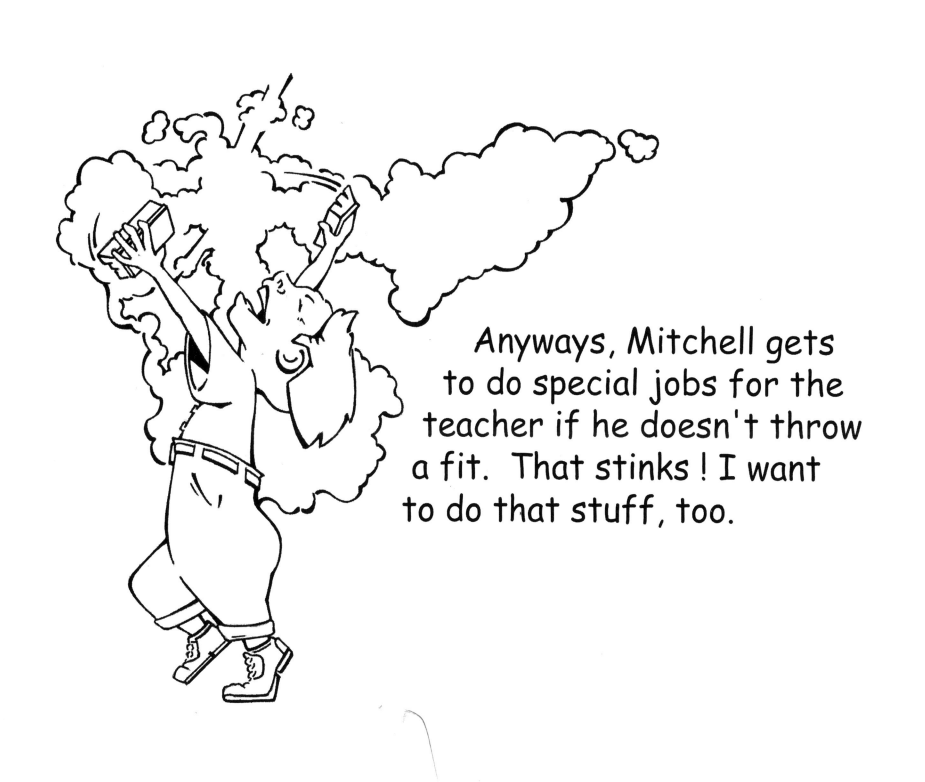

Anyways, Mitchell gets to do special jobs for the teacher if he doesn't throw a fit. That stinks ! I want to do that stuff, too.

Mitchell only comes to class in the morning lately. He mostly puts his head down and won't do anything. Then Mrs. Sherman comes and they leave.

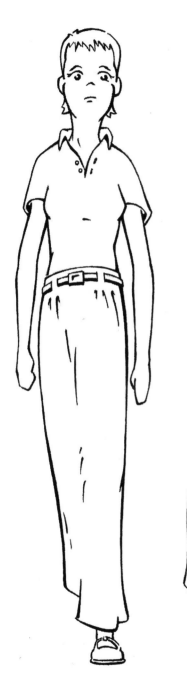

Sometimes when we go to music we can hear him crying in Mrs. Sherman's room. Once it sounded like an explosion in there. Mrs. Sherman came out into the hall and her face was all red and scrunched up. I said "hi," but I don't think she heard me.

Sometimes when Mitchell's in class Mrs. Donley looks real sad. I thought she was crying on Tuesday but that can't be, 'cause teachers don't cry. We were in computer lab and Mitchell started banging his fists on the keyboard. Real hard, like he was mad or something.

He screamed louder than my little sister Paige does when she gets a shot! I hate loud noises so I covered my ears.

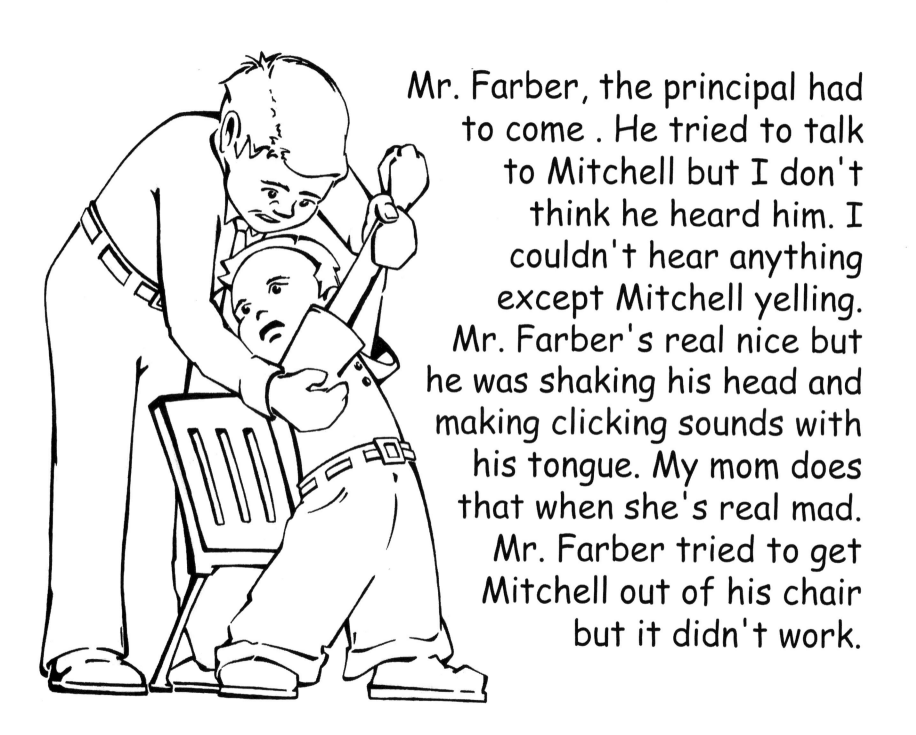

Mr. Farber, the principal had to come . He tried to talk to Mitchell but I don't think he heard him. I couldn't hear anything except Mitchell yelling. Mr. Farber's real nice but he was shaking his head and making clicking sounds with his tongue. My mom does that when she's real mad. Mr. Farber tried to get Mitchell out of his chair but it didn't work.

Mrs. Donley tried to pick Mitchell up but I think he kicked her. Maybe that's why she looked like she was crying. It must have hurt or something. Mrs. Sherman and Mrs. Parker, the nurse, came that time. Mitchell looked like a robot when they dragged him out of the lab. His legs didn't bend or anything and he covered up his face so I couldn't tell if he was crying. He sure was yelling!

Monday is Valentine's Day. That's my favorite holiday. I even made a Valentine for Mitchell so I hope he comes to school.

Mitchell didn't come to school for our Valentine party. Mrs. Donley put all of Mitchell's cards and food in a bag to go home. I wonder if he's sick or something.

Mitchell hasn't been in school for a whole week. I asked Mrs. Donley where he was and she said he wasn't feeling well. I wonder if he's got the flu or something. I once had the flu and got to stay home for four whole days. It wasn't so great 'cause my head hurt real bad. I wonder if Mitchell's head hurts.

Mitchell didn't come back to school again today. Mrs. Sherman came and took everything out of Mitchell's desk. I don't know why she did that. How was Mitchell going to do his work? Mrs. Donley didn't even say anything to Mrs. Sherman. Why was she letting her take Mitchell's stuff?

I think Mitchell is gone forever. I don't think he's coming back 'cause there's still nothing in his desk and it's in the corner of the room.

I know I was mad at Mitchell a lot, but it's weird that he's gone. I feel kind of sad but I don't know why. It's not like he was so nice.

He wasn't really a friend of mine. But I didn't hate him or anything. Maybe once I did, but that was it.

My mom said Mitchell would be in a special school now. I thought she said my school was the best school there was. I asked her why Mitchell couldn't stay at our school. She said he was having some trouble and needed extra help. I still don't really get it, but I hope Mitchell gets a friend in his new school. I would miss my friends, like Lauren and Hillary.

Today we wrote cards to Mitchell at his new school. We said we missed him, and he should write back. I'm kinda glad 'cause maybe he'll like that. I know I would. I love to get mail.

ABOUT THE AUTHOR
Karen Turkovitz earned her degree in elementary
education. She teaches the NISUS program (Nurturing Individual Strengths
and Understandings in Students) at a primary school in Rochester, NY. Karen
lives with her husband, three children, and two dogs.

ABOUT THE ILLUSTRATOR
Ian Marshall is an illustrator living in Rochester, NY. He graduated with a
Bachelor of Fine Arts Degree from S.U.N.Y. Geneseo. After spending six
years as a commercial animator, he is now completing his Masters
in Art Education at Nazareth College.

* Order Form

Price per book $ 5.50

Number of books ordered   _____

Subtotal $ _____

NY Residents 8% Tax $ _____

Shipping & Handling $ _____
(Based on weight)

Total $ _____

Print Name   _____

Address   _____

                    _____

*Send check or money order only

Mail to: Five Degrees Press
                    P.O. Box 178
                    N. Greece, NY 14515